In Morocco

رحلة امرأة أمريكية

poems by

Ellen Hernandez

Finishing Line Press
Georgetown, Kentucky

In Morocco

رحلة امرأة أمريكية

ACKNOWLEDGMENTS

My first visit to Morocco was as a tourist, a traveler marveling at its splendor, its rich culture, welcoming people, and fascinating history, journeying to the medinas, the ancient kasbahs, the family homes and local cafés, to the desert, through the mountains, and even sailing above it all in a balloon. I departed in love with every bit of it. Before the plane touched back down in America, I knew this place had taken hold of me, and I had to return as soon as I could for a deeper experience. My subsequent journey was as a lodger, a student, and a writer, a journey inward of reclaiming my lost self and a sense of equilibrium. Every day was an exploration. Mornings I went to school and afternoons I wrote—in the café, in the park, in my apartment—finally becoming the woman I had always meant to be. I would do it again.

Publisher: Leah Maines
Editor: Christen Kincaid
Cover Art: Ellen Hernandez
Author Photo: Richard Hernandez
Cover Design: Elizabeth Maines McCleavy

Printed in the USA on acid-free paper.
Order online: www.finishinglinepress.com
also available on amazon.com

Author inquiries and mail orders:
Finishing Line Press
P. O. Box 1626
Georgetown, Kentucky 40324
U. S. A.

Table of Contents

Part I—In the Village

Dust 1

Warda 2

Moroccan Men 3

In the Café 5

A Mountain Day 8

On the Road to Marrakech 10

Part II—In the City

First Shopping 11

Dakhila 13

Heat 14

Wrong Way 16

Traveler or Lodger 17

Saida 19

Small Blessings 20

Not Muslim 21

The Marketplace 22

Les Deux Freres 27

Traveling Musicians 29

Part III—Departure

Morocco 30

For Hassan and Saida

أعزائي, لقد علمتماني أن أحب لغتم و ثقافتكم و بلدم, بارك الله فيكما

ⵜⴰⵎⴰⵣⵉⵖⵜ

ⵣ

Part I—In the Village
July, Tighza, High Atlas Mountains

———————————

Dust

into the car through
open windows,
covering our bags,
our clothes,
our hair.
We wound
in and around
villages
to this *riad*,
my turret room.
The men watch football
at a bottom-of-the-hill café.
I took my tea there
with them, strangely
visible, invisible, both.
Now, in my room,
door, windows open, I hear
distant children's voices, feel
dust
still on my skin. I
don't want to wash,
could stand
on this mountain, turn to
dust,
blow away.

Warda

A small, white flower grows
in mud
on the edge of a field.
It should not bloom
here.
Soil has been upturned,
seeds sown,
grass people-trodden,
dirt rain-eroded.
The summer sun
turns soil to dust,
wind-blown
through these mountains.
Still it roots
in this spot,
ennobles
this path.

Moroccan Men

Moroccan men work
waking to sleeping,
sweating with industry,
in field, in shop,
in tannery.

Moroccan men cook.
Careful hands cut carrots,
peel potatoes for tajine,
pour mint tea,
serve gladly guests
and God.

Moroccan men pray
throughout the day,
hear the call,
set aside work
for mosque or quiet corner,
lay out a rug
and bend.
They fast at *Ramadan*,
give to the poor,
live their faith.

Moroccan men
play music together,
gather on sofa or floor
to eat, talk, drink tea.
They watch football in a café,
cheer their team's goals,
shrug off the losses.

Moroccan men
speak with kindness,
smile at strangers,
love their children
with a tender hand,
caress their faces.

Moroccan men
greet one another
with *salaam*, a hug and
kisses on the cheeks,
put hand on heart
to say goodbye.

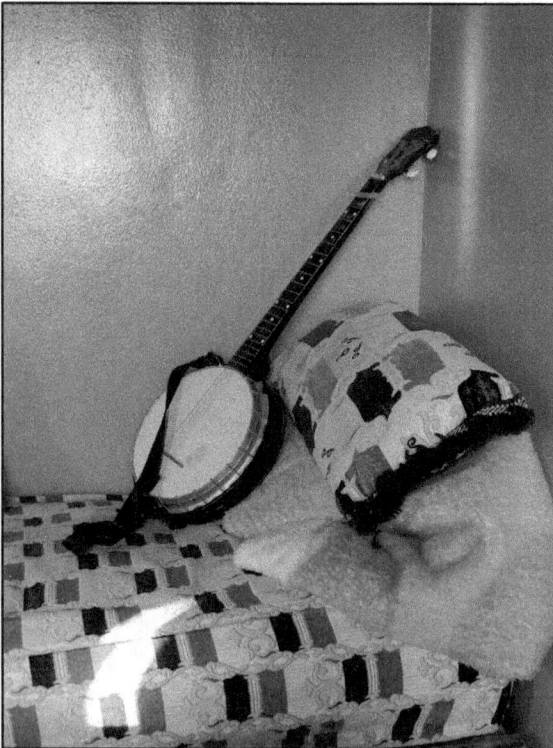

In the Café

I am in the café,
with its tv mounted
on an orange wall
for watching football.
I am the lone woman
among the village men—
seven of them—
on white plastic chairs
scraping a concrete floor.
I sip cardamom-spiced coffee
from a clear glass,
choking Marquise smoke
from card-playing men.
I do not wear a *hijab*.
I am a curiosity, but
unbothered.

Outside the door,
young Khalid scans his phone
while Youssef prays
on the ground, a rug laid,
his forehead dipping,
again, and again,
as an announcer calls the plays
and a steady buzz rises
from the stadium
like the call to prayer
of the *muezzin*.

A fly rests on my glass,
observed,
unbothered.

The café fills
as sun sets low over mountain,
the open door capturing last light.
One by one,
more men arrive,
a slow, uphill pace
to a gathering place
that smells of cigarettes,
coffee, mint tea, and orange soda,
but never *kahul*.

Two village boys
play cards in the corner,
observing and learning
how to be men.
Little Ali, a red jacket
with green *maghrib* star
draping his bony shoulders,
offers, "*Bonjour, Madame,*"
to my smile and wave.

An elder in light brown *djellaba*,
leather *babouche* slippers,
blue baseball cap
over a shock of white hair,
delights in a goal,
dances up to the screen,
motions a kiss to the team
from a toothless grin.

Ali leaps
to his sandaled feet,
cheers
an overtime goal.

Anticipation builds
at two-for-two on penalties,
each missing the third,
each getting the fourth,
a block and a win.
The café erupts,
friends chasing friends,
settling to card games,

and I ascend the steps
to a late supper.

A Mountain Day

From my bed,
I watch the white curtains
barely stirring.
My ears strain
for human noise.
Finding none, I rise.

Three villages—
mud-colored homes
blending into hills.
Choruses of chaffinches,
insistent roosters,
a single, grating donkey,
but no movement
in green fields
irrigated by lamplight
last night,
or in village streets—just
a spotted cat along a wall below.

Trudging uphill
for my morning meal,
Omar the cook
looks up at my window.
We wave.
For us,
gestures and nods
must say everything.

Downstairs, I converse with men
with bread, oil, tea, and then
listen to their tongue
and their music,
one, thrumming a banjo,
me, drumming an armrest.

Ahmed sings, and brings
to my eye
a tear
for a familiar song.

In the kitchen with Omar, I sit
at a round, brown-and-tan-tiled table,
peel and chop onions,
carrots, potatoes, peppers—
ask *saghir* or *kabir*?—small or big?—
to sauté for a *tajine*
with spice,
and dice tomatoes for salad.
We mix *aubergine* with cumin,
turmeric, honey, saffron.
We test it with torn-off bread,
spoon a few grains of boiled rice
and nod at their readiness,
alternating thank-yous—
merci, shukran, tanemmirt.

Later, for dinner, we
pick rocks from lentils,
heads inclined,
a sweet and quiet task.
More *riad* guests arrive,
soon making a too-crowded kitchen
full of talking and laughter.
English, Spanish, German, French,
Arabic, Darija, Tamazight—
we flow in and out of languages
like a mountain stream.

On the Road to Marrakech

Oleander paints
this mountain road
as Tinariwen's blues
flow from the radio.
The mellow strains
of *molo* lute,
persistent pulse
of *djembe* drum
twine tempo and tune
'round trembling moan.

I will recall
these wailing songs
and these blushing flowers,
when I am standing
on a Marrakech sidewalk.

Part II—In the City
July and August, Marrakech

First Shopping
Quartier Mabrouka

Down five flights
from flat number 9,
I exit building C,
proceed to the street,
and greet the guard,
"Marhaban."
Cross? Or turn?
He, in ball cap and
belly-stretched, white shirt,
rises from a shade tree,
approaches quizzically.
No word for grocer,
I try *"Pharmacie?"*
He points the way.

Through a blue gate,
past a bike repair,
along the avenue there,
to a produce shop—
avocado, peach, and pepper
grapes, tomatoes, a fig for later—
Onward to the grocer—
coffee, honey, water,
tuna, bread, and oil.
I ask, *"Saabuun?"*
am offered Dove
or something local.
"Sukkar saghir?"
brings sugar cubes.
Eggs are sold loose.
I buy khamsa—
a remembered number-word.

I gather my coins,
depart with *"Shukran,"*
retrace my route.

Evening's *adhan* resonates:
a bearded man faces Mecca
against a courtyard wall,
cardboard for a prayer rug.

The guard nods knowingly
as I pass
and smiles at my lighter steps,
my three swaying bags,
goods bought in Arabic,
like a triumph.

Fruit washed, stored,
coffee-water boiled,
the cup savored sweet
with one succulent fig.
Dinner is bread, olive oil,
a sliced red pepper,
a not-quite-ripe avocado.
Jamiila.

Dakhila

A McDonald's
at a roundabout
in Marrakech
where route 7 meets 9—
sleek, two stories
of steel, wood, and tinted glass—
seems strange,
dakhil.

An American woman
at a crossroads
in Marrakech—
an incongruous stranger,
fleshy and gray—
could stay,
master the language,
still never wholly belong.
Dakhila.

Heat

I step
into a courtyard,
pass a shop,
bistro and café.

I cross
the avenue,
walk on barren, rocky dirt
to a busy, shadeless boulevard
of cars and cabs,
buses, bikes, and trucks.

I pass
the men with carts
of plums and melons,
construction-equipment lots,
broken glass,
stray dogs,
a woman, babe in arms,
her head and body covered
and eyes cast down.

I enter
a *patisserie*,
scan the eclairs, tarts, *ghoribat*,
pretend to shop for sweets
just for the chilled air
in this heavy heat.

I march
past a *boucherie*,
a *pharmacie*,
an eatery,
down a side street
to a quiet cul-de-sac
with sand-colored villas

bougainvillea, zinnias,
and orange trees,
a *maghrib* guard
who nods "good-day."

I push
the heavy, metal door
climb the stairs
to a small, shaded alcove.

I rest
before my lesson,
drink cool, bottled water,
dab with a scarf my sweat,
creeping in elbow creases,
behind knees,
feel it trickle down my back.

I lament
my unavoidable smell
of sweat and dirt and pity
all during my lesson,
wishing I knew words of apology
in Arabic.

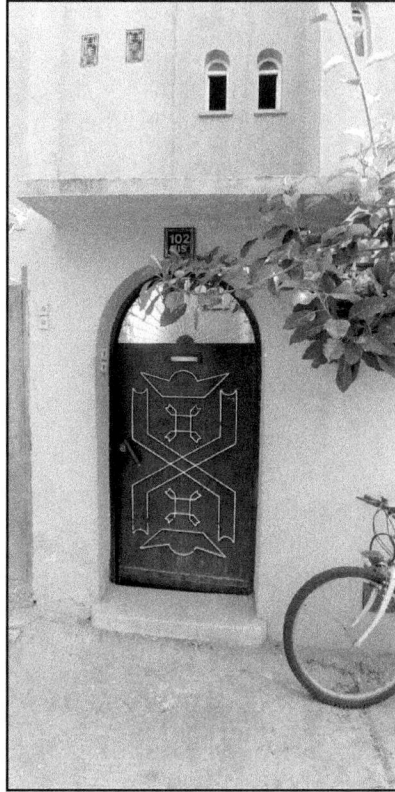

Wrong Way
Gueliz

Discovering bus 15
at Avenue Abdel Ghanem
I murmur *alHamdu-lillah!*

Later, light-headed
from the heat
and a two-hours lesson,
I board the number 1
in the wrong direction.

Disoriented,
I find myself
in Gueliz,
adjust,
and leisurely lunch on couscous
in a cool room
with white tablecloths.

Then, I board the bus
back
the other way.

Traveler or Lodger
Jardin Majorelle

The crowded Saturday bus
to Ben Tbib in Rouidate
was market-day standing-only.

At Jardin Majorelle,
I mix Arabic, English, French
for the concession clerk—
"assalaamu alaykum, bonjour, hello,"
and am welcomed.
The ticket-taker at the gate
points to my forearm tattoo—
yaz for the Imazighen,
the free people—
smiles, pats my shoulder
in solidarity.

Sitting in the garden
beside a trickling fountain,
observing passersby,
listening to visitors, their languages.
I enjoy this pretending
to be a tourist,
not a lodger.

I photograph the details—
fountain, flowers,
lanterns, planters,
the chalkboard café menu—
lunching French Moroccan:
mango juice,
bread with oil,
red pepper soup,
raisins and beets
with ginger and orange,
cumin-coriandered eggplants,
parsleyed lentils,
pickled peppers and tomatoes.

Tourist prices,
yet I eat like a local,
friend-taught to scoop
with bread
from my right hand.
A young Spaniard
at a nearby table
witnesses my manner,
averts his embarrassed eyes.
To myself,
I smile
like a contented *medina* cat.
My oil-and-spice-fragranced fingers,
in truth,
are pleasure-giving.

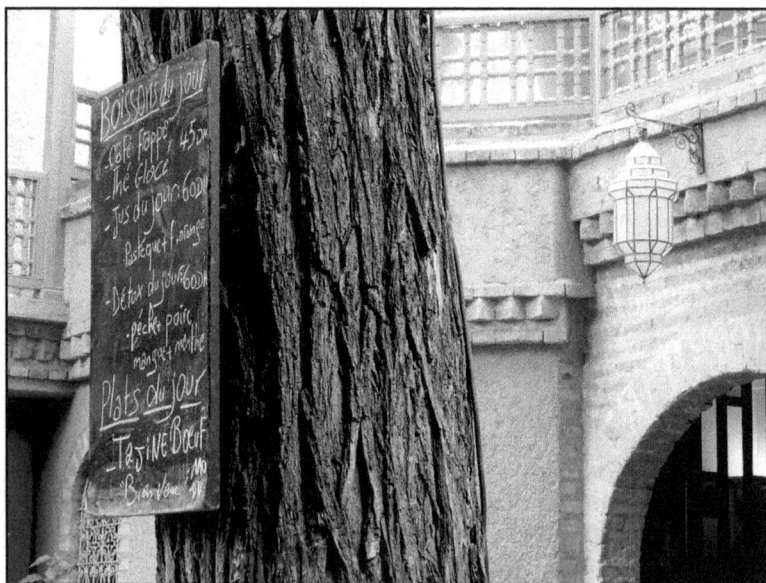

Saida

Café Amine

Saida—
sweet as *sukkar*—
says *ladayk qalb latif,*
"You have a kind heart."

Between-lesson topics
fill our breaks
over full cups of *qahwa*—
'amrika, almaghrib,
taelim, taealam,
aldiyn, alHuriyat,
alhijrat, alqadr.

I draw a map;
she asks about cities—
D.C., New York, and Miami.
"Where do the Muslims live?"
she asks,
her lovely face
embraced by her *hijab.*

I want to use her words,
want to learn and remember,
to hear her say,
"*Jayyid.*"
Good.

Small Blessings
Café Allal

A bus held by a red light,
a rescue from the creeping heat,
lingers for me.

An open window where I stand
closed-eyed among the crowd
offers a breeze.

A mother's eyes under a scarf,
after an infant's kiss,
meet mine
and we share a knowing smile.

A shade-cooled café
grants time and canopy,
for a croissant and a coffee.

Not Muslim

Lessane Arabi Center

Saida serves me *qahwa*
on our break,
enjoying quietly
our *tartes fine du pommes*
from Amoud Patisserie,
and the midday *adhan* call:
Allahu 'akbar!
Hayya 'alaa aSSalaah!

We talk of charity,
of modesty,
of abstaining from pork
and alcohol.
She asks,
"Why you are not Muslim?"

I cannot explain,
for I do not know
myself.

The Marketplace
Jemaa' el-fnaa

Checking my phone
while awaiting a morning taxi,
I nearly nudge a dead cat
and her kitten
decomposing in dried grass
under the African sun,
a mouth still clinging to a mother's belly
for the milk that would not come.

After Arabic lessons,
I take a bus to the marketplace.
Two women join me
on a low concrete wall
for the long wait,
and motion its arrival.
Closed, stifling,
any papers become fans.
Young, covered women
gesture and nod with *laa*—
no, not yet—
once, twice, a third time,
to keep me still until my stop:
Koutoubia Mosque,
near *almadiinat.*

Past the busses,
the taxis and tourists,
alHudhiuwn and their horse-drawn carriages
in three queues along the colonnade,
I enter the massive marketplace—
Jemaa' el-fnaa—
crowded on the sabbath,
a Friday afternoon.

Dodging the sellers,
the snake charmers,
the henna artists,

the monkey handlers,
the musicians,
the poor and the addicted,
I skirt the vendor-clustered edges,
with purpose,
in a singular direction.

I round the corner,
past oranges, mangoes, melons,
as each seller beckons.
I feel the juice from tobacco,
warm and black,
trail down my ankle
into blue canvas shoes.
Inside Café Argana,
past the doorman,
the elegant, brass fittings,
the *patisserie* display,
I take a napkin,
stoop to wipe my leg
before ascending
the marble steps.

Seated on the balcony,
I face the square.
A lunch of green olives,
harissa-spiced,
and salad *niçoise*,
I watch the shoppers—
locals and tourists alike—
and the night-sellers,
setting their metal poles
and canvas canopies:
a vantage point
from which to write.

From here, the whole
displayed for me,
all music and rhythms
of this mass of humanity,
the great, giddy hum of life.

Afterwards, I cross the square,
scooters zooming diagonally past
the ever-increasing swarm.
A cheap paperback
from a bookshop-browse,
some bracelets, two postcards,
a two-sided *tabla* drum,
a small Amazigh doll,
with faded pink dress:
for these I haggle
to one third what is asked—
"No! *Laa*! the Moroccan's price."

Dusk descends.
Winding my way among the souks,
harangued by hawkers,

I wave them away
with *laa, shukran,*
until I spot it.
Two nights we ate here in a row
four months ago,
an eyelid-shutting, lip-licking soup.
I find a seat,
remove straw hat, sunglasses,
am recognized, with delight,
served a bowl
from a giant metal tureen,
I declare it *bnin,*
pleasing Aziz.

Past Saharan musicians,
I stop for dates.
"*Jumaa Mubarak*"—good sabbath—
surprises and pleases the seller,
who bestows a spiced-nut handful,
a parting gift.

Outside the square, I wait
for bus 15,
a girl-child and a grandmother,
beside me on the bench,
curious at my Fatima bracelet,
the *yaz* tattoo against my pale skin.
The *jidda's* eyes widen
at this symbol of the free people,
points to it, then to herself,
a wrinkled hand to heart,
a sparkle in her eyes,
warm smile, and nod of solidarity.

My camera shoots
the passing traffic:
yellow petit taxis, motorbikes,
cars, trucks, donkey-led carts—
as people weave in and between.
Soon, I tire of the wait,
step from the curb, negotiate.
Through the cab's window,
I cast a backward gaze,
am bid goodbye with friendly waves.

Outside the window,
almadiinat retreats,
we zip through Gueliz,
and I reject an American tune—
"Something Moroccan, please"—
and sit back
to enjoy the breeze.

Les Deux Freres
Quartier Mabrouka

At a table for two,
outdoors,
I sit alone,
with a carafe of water,
a cruet of olive oil.
American and Moroccan music mix
as cars and bikes scoot by.
Flies are everywhere,
immune to swatting,
landing on
the brown table,
the small glass,
the plate of pasta,
the napkin,
my shoulder.

A woman in floral head scarf
and peach caftan
eats French fries
with her curly-headed little boy
in shorts, shirt, and sandals,
playing with a police car
and Spiderman toy.
An elderly man
in white, pinstriped shirt,
grey trousers,
waits patiently in a chair
for his takeout order.
Delivery boys and wait staff
come and go
past all of us.

My bill is a long-time-coming,
Morocco's pace made sluggish
by sultry air.
Staring across the street
at buildings of cinnamon and ginger,

I lazily linger,
listen to a singer
vowing to stay with me
only one more night.

A boy in Moroccan football shirt
silently scanning his cell phone
sits atop a two-tiered pallet—
home gas containers for sale.

I stare for awhile
at a fly resting on my wrist.
Under the next table,
a tabby cat creeps
for shade or food.

Traveling Musicians

Residence Najd

Blue sky and sunlight
seep through
my curtained windows.
Lying in bed,
I listen
for the daily constant
of nearby construction,
the banging of steel girders,
of mallet on wedge
pounding bricks into place.

In the courtyard below,
two turbaned Tuaregs—
one with handheld *bendir* drum,
the other a double-reed *ghraita* flute—
walk the streets
playing for money.

A boy hands coins
through a locked gate.
A protest—inadequate—a heated exchange:
the boy escapes.
Their gaze is raised
to my fifth-floor window.
Waving,
I close the window,
and retreat.

Part III—Departure
August, Menara Airport

Morocco

Morocco, you welcomed me
with warm smiles
beneath honey dark eyes.
You said *salaam* and summoned me
with the call of the *muezzin*,
like the collective hum of honeybees.
Now, you cling to my bones
like the mud-straw walls of the *kasbah*.

Morocco, you comforted me
like the embrace of the *hijab*,
like the morning lark-song.
You are the Saharan sand in my hair,
the shadow on the dunes.
You are a bright, desert sunrise,
stinging my eyes—
the *tbilat* drum
still pounding in my ears.

Morocco,
you are the sticky-sweet date,
the glass of mint tea,
the sugar cube between my teeth.
You are spiced olives on my tongue,
warm, fresh bread dipped in argan oil.
You are a *tajine*
eaten in a family home,
crossed legs on a carpet,
the sound of laughter

and clanging of kitchen pots.
You are a prayer whose words catch in my throat.

Morocco,
I drink you like the springs of the Sacred Fish.
I inhale you like the Atlas air.
You are the winding roads of a map
drawn on my skin.
You are the grazing mountain sheep
in whose shorn wool I wrap myself.

Morocco,
leaving you breaks my heart
like the split *aljuyudat* for sale
along the highway.
In my dreams, I search
the labyrinthine alleys
of the madiinat.
Only when I find myself there
drinking *qahwa* in a café
will I have peace again.

Additional Acknowledgments

Grateful acknowledgement is made to the many friends, colleagues, and extended family who supported my summer sabbatical, especially to Prof. Keith O'Shaughnessy for the feedback that shaped the final draft; the thousands of students who have passed through my classroom doors who inspire me to continue to learn; my mother, brother, and sister—each of whom sent me off on a wild adventure with probably more uneasiness than they let on but who tried not to let it show; my late father for his sage advice; and, finally, for all good things in life, my unending love to husband Richard and daughter Mia, who make everything possible.

I extend special thanks to the people of Morocco who welcomed me with kindness and generosity of spirit. In particular, I thank the hosts at the Riad Kasbah Oliver and the people of Tighza village, Mohammed Ennouichi of Café Clock, the Lessane Arabi Center, my teacher Saida Zamkhoukh, and my friend Hassan Hisse, for his invaluable assistance.

Ellen Hernandez first traveled to Morocco in early 2018, returning four months later to study Arabic, maintain an online blog, and write poetry, resulting in this collection. She has taught English for over thirty years. She holds a B.A. in English Literature and Linguistics and a Master's in English Literature and Education. She is the co-author of *Portfolios: A Guide for Writing Students* (McGraw-Hill) and author of *Writing for All* (2nd edition, Cognella, Inc., 2019) as well as the chapter "*Downton Abbey*, the Jazz Age, and Adaptation to Change" in *Exploring Downton Abbey: Critical Essays* (Scott Stoddard, ed., McFarland & Co., 2018). *In Morocco* is her first collection of poetry. She lives in southern New Jersey with her family.

Grateful acknowledgement is made to the many friends, colleagues, and extended family who supported her summer sabbatical, especially to Prof. Keith O'Shaughnessy for the feedback that shaped the final draft; the thousands of students who have passed through her classroom doors who inspire her to continue to learn; her mother, brother, and sister—each of whom sent her off on a wild adventure with probably more uneasiness than they let on but who tried not to let it show; her late father for his sage advice; and, finally, for all good things in life, her unending love to husband Richard and daughter Mia, who make everything possible.

She extends special thanks to the people of Morocco who welcomed her with kindness and generosity of spirit, particularly to Hassan Hisse and Saida Zamkhoukh—eaziziha—who taught her to love their language, their culture, and their country.